Creating the French Look

Creating the French Look

inspirational ideas and 25 step-by-step projects

annie sloan

CICO BOOKS
LONDON NEW YORK

First edition published in 2008 by CICO Books
This paperback edition published in 2011 by CICO Books
an imprint of Ryland Peters & Small Ltd

20–21 Jockey's Fields   519 Broadway, 5th Floor
London WC1R 4BW   New York, NY 10012

www.cicobooks.com

10 9 8 7 6 5 4

A CIP catalog record for this book is available from the Library of
Congress and the British Library.

ISBN-13: 978 1 907563 95 9

Printed in China

Project Editor: Robin Gurdon
Designer: David Fordham
Photographer: Christopher Drake

contents

introduction

The distinct French sense of design in food, fashion, and interiors has had a profound effect on the rest of the world. Since the beginning of the 18th century right through to the present day it has continued to cast its spell over us. France has led the way not only in design but also in fine art. The most influential artists of the 20th century came from France, and Paris was the creative pulse at the center of it all.

It is difficult to define what French taste is and why it has continued to be so popular. For interiors, the best description is probably subtlety and simplicity but with flair. The style tends to be unadorned and crisp, the emphasis on less being more. In many other cultures, minimalism can become gruffly basic and crude; in French hands it is graceful and balanced with just the right amount of decoration and shapeliness. French style is playful and delicate—never heavy, never over-adorned, and never complicated. The curve of even the plainest

ABOVE
What better way to say France and, in particular, Paris than designers' mannequins, here re-covered in vintage linen.

ABOVE RIGHT
Decorative buttons draw attention to the clever use of striped fabric in these pillows to create a simple cross motif.

LEFT

The simplicity of French style is summed up by the plain linen of a curtain edged with decorative braid, combined with the delicate and subtle colors of a hydrangea in a white pitcher.

chair leg has a sense of proportion and balance. Even at its grandest, furniture may be ornate but the color will be very quiet.

In this book we have tried to bring together the elements of French style to help you achieve the look in your own home. We did not photograph in France but in the homes of people who know and love France, buy French furniture or paint reproduction pieces, and love good-quality materials. So rest assured the basic starting point does not need to be a fine farmhouse in Provence.

Just as French cuisine uses basic but very fresh ingredients so it is with interior design. Polyester, plastic, and fiber board won't do. Instead, fine cottons and linens, and natural materials such as metal, wood, stone, and terra cotta should be combined with matt paints rather than shiny, artificial finishes. France has never been a throwaway culture, so bear in mind the idea of adaptation and reuse is part of the country's tradition.

ABOVE

A simple country-style, painted kitchen is given the French look with details such as the painted plates and the hooks for hanging pots and pans. Vintage dish towels look wonderful and are practical because linen absorbs water so well.

Part One

the looks

elements of French style

To help explain the wealth of decorative styles that France has given us, I have divided the history of French interior design by period and region, whether urban or rural. While this might be a little arbitrary—there is obviously a lot of crossover between the different areas—it is a good way to begin to understand the essential ingredients of French design styles, including colors and fabrics. Each of the photographs on the following pages includes more or less the same components for château, country, Provençal, and Parisian styles. This makes it easier to see the unique combination of colors, fabrics, and materials that are used to create a particular look.

Historically, two main design movements originated in France. The extravagant rococo and the austere neo-classical styles developed either side of the extraordinary intellectual, political, and artistic upheaval that surrounded the French Revolution. Both were extremely influential across Europe, and feature everywhere from the French farmhouse to Parisian apartment.

The following style photographs also reflect the way in which French country society was highly stratified with houses ranked as *manoir*, *maison gentilhomme*, *maison de maître*, and *maison bourgeois* over and above the simple farmhouse and cottage. The *manoir* might be an owner's country retreat for the summer or the home of an aspiring merchant, so the style would be quite different from a working farmhouse interior.

The French urban look has come to mean the chic and bohemian sophistication of the capital city. Paris is still a city of culture and design, but its boom time was in the first half of the 20th century. Although there is a lot of crossover, Parisian style can be broadly divided into the cultivated and refined *haute couture* look and the hip, even a little racy, bohemian interior.

ABOVE

The Council Chamber at Versailles was designed by Ange-Jacques Gabriel under the direction of Louis XV. Enormous crystal chandeliers, huge mirrors, and soft white-painted paneling with gilded asymmetrical garlands, shell-like motifs, and molding epitomize the delicate rococo style that continues to influence interior design nearly 300 years later.

LEFT

In contrast, the neo-classical design of Napoleon's bedroom at the Château de Malmaison in Paris is simplicity itself. It looks modern but was designed about 50 years after the rococo rooms at Versailles. Symmetry and formality are the main elements. The most popular French design style today is a combination of flowing rococo and classical structure.

Weather has also played an important role in the development of French interior design styles. France is a huge country and the climate in the north is quite different from that in the south. North of the Loire there are no vineyards because the winters are cold and the summers, though long, are mild rather than hot. This calls for more indoor living, with warm fabrics and furniture influenced by Paris and the château. As you head south towards the Riviera the weather becomes increasingly warm. Here outdoor living has led to a more exotic style, influenced by colorful and intricate fabrics, ironwork and wood carving from Spain and North Africa, accessible via Marseilles.

1 Château – Rococo
Pretty and sparkling

CHANDELIER – A crystal chandelier is the essence of this style, giving both a magnificent focus to a room as well as sparkle and delicacy. There are a lot of chandeliers available today from vintage to brand new.

EMBROIDERED LINEN SHEET AND LACE – Linen sheets and pillowcases were once part of every French girl's trousseau. They would be lovingly initialled in embroidery, all ready for the marriage bed. Tablecloths with lace edges and ladder work were also part of the dowry. Continue to use them today as bed sheets or turn them into curtains, pillows or lampshades.

TOILE DE JOUY – This fabric design is uniquely French. Use it as a wall covering, for upholstery or curtains. The designs often have literary and mythological references and are now usually printed in a single color on off-white cotton. Originally they could have been multi-colored and perhaps have Chinese or Indian designs.

SILKS AND PLAIN-COLORED LINENS – The château would have silks and fine brocades as well as tapestries. Today it is often preferable to replace busy tapestries with simple linens.

BRAID – Search flea markets for fine vintage *passementerie*, in the form of tassels, braids, and ropes to add to the edges of curtain, pillows, and upholstery. Many new braids are also available to add that finishing touch.

PAINTWORK – Woodwork was very often painted. Old White and Paris Grey are the best colors to choose to recreate the look. After painting furniture, doors, and other woodwork, distress lightly and add a little gold in some places.

MIRRORS – Like chandeliers, mirrors add light and sparkle, so use as many as possible in as large a size as you can, preferably with a decorative scroll-like design.

GILDING – A touch of gold on mirrors and on the molding of painted doors and furniture enhances elegance.

2 Château – Neo-classical
Bold, military, shiny

THE EAGLE MIRROR – Decorative symbols, including animals, that signify power and strength are key to the neo-classical look. Lions and eagles were popular motifs, used on mirrors, furniture, and table and chair legs. The bee, symbol of industry, was common, as were stars and laurel leaves. Mirrors make a grand statement as do other classical elements, such as urns, obelisks, and columns. Favored furniture includes *bateau lits* and canopy daybeds as well as secretaires and campaign-style chairs.

COLORS – Search out bold and rich colors for walls and fabrics. Use Antibes Green, Riviera Blue or Burgundian Red paint or fabric on the walls. Combine these strong colors with lots of white—flowing white curtains, the only soft line in this style, are very effective—black, and gold.

FABRICS – Use transparent voiles for windows and striped fabrics to drape tent-like over beds, or hang over four posters. Upholster furniture with damasks and checkered fabrics as well as rich, heavy silks.

MATERIALS – Gold-colored metals, marble, and woods predominate. Military symbols of spears and shields and metal studs decorate wall-mounted candelabra.

LIMOGES PLATE –The deep green border of laurel leaves is a typically symmetrical design. Look out for white porcelain with a gold border.

3 Country – *Manoir*
Delicate and stylish

CHANDELIERS AND WALL-MOUNTED LIGHTING – These are most likely to be made of wood and painted. Paris Grey, used here, with touches of gold is characteristic. They can be left as decorative candle holders or wired for electric lights with translucent candle-shaped lamps.

TOILE DE JOUY – Some *toile de Jouy* is very grand but later designs include nostalgic country scenes, such as Victorian children playing by the sea, as shown here.

QUILTED BED COVERS – Called a *boutis* when sewn with scalloped edges, these are made from flowery fabrics as well as *toiles* with pastoral scenes. Such fabrics can be used in the living room as well as the bedroom, depending on the color scheme and design. For curtains and pillows in keeping with the look, find both coarse and fine linens in antique markets or *brocantes*.

FRENCH PORCELAIN – Examples decorated with flowers, garlands, and just a touch of gold work well with the floral *boutis* and *toile de Jouy*.

COLOR – Whites, very pale ochers, County Cream and putty grays form the base note, and you can add interest to cupboard interiors or small walls with simple stenciling.

SIMPLICITY – With so many patterns, keep the look uncluttered by painting furniture white, then distressing it. Think of a painted country *armoire* filled with lovely linens or china.

4 Country – Rural
Simple and homey

GINGHAM FABRIC – Red and blue gingham fabric, with large or small squares, is a good way to begin this style. Use it to make gathered curtains or pillows.

WHITE LINEN – Use white linen without elaborate embroidery for bed sheets or bedroom curtains. Faded stripes work well but try not to use too much pattern. White lace borders on *armoires* look very pretty.

KITCHEN DETAILS – The kitchen is the main living area in rural houses. Old kitchen pieces, such as blue and white china with simple stenciled or hand-painted designs, can be found in markets across France. Also search out enamelware coffee pitchers, old coffee grinders, and baskets. Vintage French dish towels are a must to use for their original purpose, or to make pillows or lampshades, or to upholster chairs.

PINE – Wash plain pine furniture with a light gray or Old White paint so that the wood is given a patinated look while the grain is still apparent. Very distressed paintwork, with the paint rubbed away to reveal a lot of wood, is also effective.

COLORS – Whites of all sorts are essential for this look, from a pale whitewashed effect to thick creamy paintwork. Blues and reds are a must but also consider chocolate browns and other warm colors.

FABRIC DETAILS – Interesting braids and edgings, such as a rope design or vintage blue and white border, are the finishing touches needed for this simple and generally patternless style.

STONE SURFACES – Keep textures matt with terra-cotta tiles and roughly hewn stone floors.

5 Provence – Luberon
Bright, airy and fresh

LAVENDER – This is an ever-present *leitmotif* in the home, the yard, and the countryside. Think of pots of lavender in the house and yard, a lavender motif on fabrics, lavender colored accessories and lavender bags for their beautiful scent. The soft green gray of olive trees is another reminder of the smoky colors of Provence.

OCHER – After lavender, earthy yellow ochers are probably the most significant hues seen in this part of France. This color can be seen on walls inside and out, as well as on pottery. Earthy terra cotta reds are also popular throughout the region.

POTTERY – The traditional pottery of the area is decorated with the yellow and green glazes seen on this vase. Find antique pieces, as well as terra cotta, for both the garden and your interiors.

TERRA COTTA AND STONE – Allow your interiors to merge with the outdoors in a seamless way. Terra cotta or stone floors spread from the house to the garden, bringing the two together ready for a warm summer.

FABRICS – Ensure fabric colors are soft and in keeping with those of the countryside. Whites work especially well—floor-length voile curtains over open windows, plain linens, and simple floral patterns. There are also traditional Indian-inspired cotton fabrics from Provence decorated with small flowers and paisley patterns.

THE CICADA – Also known as the cigale, the cicada is the symbol of Provence perhaps because it so clearly evokes the feeling of summer when it is heard. Find the motif on fabrics and pottery.

COLORS – Due to the predominance of ocher and terra cotta, other colors are generally kept quite soft and undemanding. A small accent of turquoise or bright green helps to keep a room from being too quiet.

PAINTWORK – Colors for paintwork include whites as well as grays, and Faded Violet or blue. Give paint a rustic texture by softly distressing it to allow a background color to show through. Add Faded Violet and Luberon Yellow furniture and accessories to help give the style a natural look.

6 Provence – Riviera
Vibrant and fresh

VEGETATION – The pronounced shape of leafy palm-tree fronds as well as dotty yellow mimosa, purple and pink bougainvillea, and other colorful plants are the backdrop to both the region and the design style. This means that the style features lots of greens, as well as other natural colors, and strong architectural shapes. These need to be integrated into interiors, so don't be shy of colors or shapes with big impact.

LINENS – The proximity of the Italian border ensures that colorful linens, decorated with stripes or in solid herringbone weaves, add a smart touch to the design style—perfect for the casino life. Mix them with modern cotton fabrics decorated with bold flowers or the French rooster and the look is clean and contemporary.

POTTERY – The Riviera is a mix of the arty and the sophisticated so decide whether you want to emphasize the natural tones and textures of the contemporary pottery pitcher or the colorful, slight sheen of the china bowl. Try mixing styles, adding contemporary furniture.

PAINTWORK – Summer blue skies, azure seas, and clear light hint at the colors needed for Riviera-style interiors. Be inspired by the Impressionists' use of bright, powerful blues toned with grays and whites. Barcelona Orange also looks terrific and punchy as long as there is plenty of white. Match with cool, summery deep lime and Riviera Blue for china, curtains and tablecloths.

MOSAICS – Tiles in shades of blue or terra cotta can be used for kitchens, bathrooms, and pools, with stone and marble tiles for floors and walls.

7 Paris – Bohemian
Artistic and eclectic

FABRICS – Be adventurous and unconventional and use fabrics such as this one, which combines a 1960s style print with South Seas Island colors. Boldly colored stripes could also work.

COLOR – Bohemian colors are vigorous but always controlled. The two main tones are blue and brown. Accents are provided by shades ranging from purple through moody pinks and red to orange—the complementary hue to blue. Blacks, whites, and neutral earthy browns help to steady the palette.

POTTERY – The purple pitcher is a resolute statement, not only in color but also in shape.

ARTIFACTS – African items, Javanese dolls or Chinese parasols give a worldly, arty look as long as they are in the right colors. Here we have a comb from Ghana and a beaded bowl from South Africa.

PICTURES – Find prints by favorite artists, such as this one by Gauguin. The black frame is neat and has a sheen. The look is mainly matt but it can combine sheen as long as the color is right.

PAINTWORK – Use anything and everything—the distressed Duck Egg Blue over Scandinavian Pink is ideal. Find old pieces of furniture as basic or refined as you want and paint them.

8 Paris – Coco *Haute Couture*
Fine design and *fin de siecle*

FABRICS – Fine voiles and cottons for floor-length curtains in white to soften the light are essential. Fabrics for upholstery are discreetly patterned, either incorporating small motifs or a minimal amount of a bold Chinoiserie or paisley design. Matelot-style stripes have a touch of gentle whimsy that works well.

COLORS – Base a scheme around black or navy and white but with powerful accents such as red. The style can be as grand as you want to make it, so add gold details too.

LIGHTING – The gold-colored chandelier has the wheatsheaf design so beloved of Coco Chanel. Look out for reproductions of this type of design along with similar styles, such as those using palm tree motifs.

PAINTS – Imitate Chinese lacquer on console tables or bureaux. Red Beret and Graphite Black, waxed and distressed, create the perfect look.

DETAILS – Using large and interesting buttons, ribbons and braid on pillows, curtains, lampshades, and upholstery is essential for this look. Also find a place for pearls, perhaps as a braid.

ARTIFACTS – A *fin de siecle* bust has the right romance and *élan* for an haute couture mantelpiece. Search for new and reproduction busts, especially large, eye-catching pieces, in garden centers and markets.

PHOTOGRAPHS – Black and white photographs look stylish in simple black frames. Search through old albums or find a poster from the 1940s or '50s to achieve the right look.

Part Two

the rooms

chapter 1

Living Room

The bergere *chair was first made in the early 18th century, partly influenced by newly imported Chinese chairs with low, rounded backs. The shape of this wooden-framed and padded chair has since been adapted in many different ways according to region and fashion. The gold paintwork of this particular example—a* bergere en gondole—*has been covered in Old White, which has then been rubbed away over the flower and shell carvings. Fully upholstered in a dark gray silk, it is edged with tacks rather than braid or piping.*

Château

Versailles and the great aristocratic houses of the 18th century have given us a lasting legacy of elegant living. It is thanks to this period of French history that the central feature of today's living rooms remains the comfortable, upholstered furniture developed for the *salon*.

ROCOCO ELEMENTS

The *salon* was softened with fabrics and its furniture was given a rounded shape. The wood used for furniture and paneling was lightened with paint and glittered with gold embellishments that were reflected in chandeliers and mirrors. Comfort was introduced as it had become fashionable to recline rather than sit upright in hard chairs. Low, wide chairs with pillows and upholstered backs and sides were introduced. Fabric colors were lighter and brighter. Designs on fabric and porcelain were mostly pastoral scenes with milkmaids, and romantic figures from mythology. The style is recognizable from any *grand salon*.

THE *BERGERE* CHAIR

The *bergere* chair epitomizes the French way of decorating more than any other piece of furniture, and

LEFT
This simple, linen-covered bergere *chair is painted white in the style of the 18th century. To combine whites successfully, different textures, from paint to voile, silk, and linen, were used to give depth. White paint would often have gilded moldings and carvings. The rest of the room has the Italianate influences found particularly around the Riviera. The table is covered in a matt damask patterned fabric with a protective sheet of glass. Ingeniously, the lamp base has been given a marble effect by covering it with marbled paper.*

its influence can be felt from the château to the country *manoir* and village house. *Bergere* literally means "shepherdess," a name that comes from rococo pastoral fantasy.

The *bergere* chair has been so successful because it can take on so many different interpretations. It is essentially wooden framed with a padded back and cushioned seat. It may have caned sides, or it may be open. It may be a small, rounded tub chair, a medallion backed open one, or be wide and fully padded with arms. Different styles have been given names such as *bergere marquise* or *bergere en gondole* but, whatever the particular style, the essential characteristic is the padded upholstery.

There are many regional variations. For instance, the Provençal style in the south is likely to have a curved ladder back with a simple, open carving, such as a basket full of flowers, while the *canapé*—a long chair resembling a padded settle—may have open or closed sides and looks very dignified.

ABOVE & ABOVE LEFT
A bergere chair in the neo-classical style has been covered in beautiful soft white but coarse-grained sack linen with double piping and brass and black studs. The curvy cabriole legs of the earlier rococo style have been replaced by straight column-like legs, and, in another architectural reference, the back is shield-shaped rather than rounded.

The robust floral fabric of this comfortable chair complements the rural subject of the painting hanging above it.

FAR RIGHT
This 19th century, neo-classical painted daybed, decorated with softly carved flowers, combines a French mattress with a simple box frame. It is covered in an elegant silky fabric with an array of silk and linen pillows, including the traditional bolsters down each side.

Other items of furniture that would have been deemed necessary in the *salon* were the console table, the commode, and the bureau. Of these, the console table has found popularity again in recent years. We like it nowadays because it allows us to keep things tidy when we try to declutter our homes. The console is essentially a long narrow table with *cabriole* legs and a shaped front or top. It often has a central drawer. There are simple Provençal examples or fancier ones with marble tops and bases made from painted ironwork.

ADAPTING ROCOCO STYLE

To recreate, or at least to take elements from, this rather feminine rococo style, the chair is probably the best starting point. The original 18th-century chairs are beyond the pocket of most of us but, fortunately, many more affordable new reproductions are on the market. The original chairs would have had tapestry or silk brocade coverings, either striped or plain, but these days we are as likely to cover them in anything from tickings to toiles or even rough linens. Although this is not historically accurate, that should not stop us—it's good to know and understand the history of

a style but it is a shame to feel restricted by it. Fashion changes as our needs change and new products become available.

The tradition of lining walls with fabric is probably more prevalent in France than in other countries, and the technique has been used in houses from the grandest château in the Loire to the *maison de maître* in a village. The idea developed in the 18th century, as part of the Rococo idea of comfort, when expensive tapestries, damasks, and silks were being made, partly influenced by hand-painted and embroidered Chinese silk as well as

cotton fabrics and Kashmiri designs from India. It softens the room as sound is absorbed by the fabric. These days northern France, where linen used to be produced, has a thriving fabric industry again, as does Lyons, where silk was traditionally made. A formal effect can be achieved by covering rigid panels in fabric and attaching them to battens, or tacking fabric directly to battens, with or without padding. The battens are then hung from special attachments, which are widely available in France. This method makes covering walls with fabric relatively easy. However, the style is also particularly good for creating an

RIGHT
Two tones of the same color give this neo-classical style table a characteristic look. Over a solid turquoise blue base, a thinned-down deeper gray blue paint has been dragged to give depth to the color. The original classical carving looks distressed and is emphasized with gold to give it the necessary rich look. The strong but dusky cerise pink of the carpet provides a lively contrast to the table.

informal impression because, when applied directly, the fabric always molds itself to the contours of the wall.

NEO-CLASSICAL ELEGANCE

When the decorative rococo style became too frothy, towards the end of the 18th century, it gave way to the uncluttered and more severe neo-classical look. This introduced the classical daybed with high, *bateau*-style sides, and the *chaise longue*, or long chair, often with round, Ottoman-style bolster pillows. These chairs may not seem particularly luxurious to those of us used to lounging on modern sofas but wide, upholstered versions can be very comfortable. Curvy *cabriole* legs were replaced by fluted columns, and console tables became less decorative and more architecturally inspired.

LUXURIOUS COLOR

Neo-classical color was lively and intense in comparison to the soft, pastel tones of the rococo period. Bright greens, rich blues, lilac pinks, and claret reds were used on walls and fabrics, with plenty of black and white for emphasis. Grand materials and references were used to enhance the feeling of affluence. One of the secrets of achieving the rich and luxurious look was the use of gold.

This is not a shy, mousey style but one that demands attention, so be prepared to make a statement with shape or color. For a contemporary interpretation of neo-classical think of the modern designer Versace. This is a style that shouts grandeur and opulence.

ABOVE
Elements of many influences are evident here but the underlying style is neo-classical. The console table and the urn on a pedestal in front of a large mirror all have strong architectural design features. The grand statement is made in typical French style by putting a large object in front of a mirror.

Country

The style of château living naturally filtered down to the manors and *gentillehomme* residences of villages and countryside, where the basic furniture of the peasant farmer met the refined embellishments of the château. However, while *manoirs* may have had separate living rooms, in farmhouses this would have been rare. The living area was much more likely to be incorporated in a large kitchen, although a separate dining room was not unusual.

Characteristic of country living spaces is the *armoire*, which, like the *bergere* chair, is a quintessentially French piece of furniture. The *armoire* often has shelves inside for keeping linen, china or other household items, and is used in the kitchen, dining room, and bedroom as well as the living room. Although usually a country piece, an *armoire* can nevertheless be very fine, and well-made examples can be found with intricate carvings.

CLEVER COLORS

While the *armoire* was originally often painted, especially in the north east of France, it could also be made in fruitwood and polished. However, this look is not popular today. Painting *armoires* in light colors makes them look smaller and helps to bring out the shape of moldings and carvings, especially with the help of some light distressing. The very oldest and highly decorated *armoires* are expensive but it is possible to buy reproductions, or new ones, cheaply to paint.

In Provence and many country areas the *armoire* was often painted in one color on the outside and another on the inside. Blues of all kinds were popular—possibly because it was thought that the color repelled flies. Whether or not this is true, soft powdery blues and duck egg greens look particularly pleasing when you open up a light brown or gray cupboard to reveal the interior. Red, yellow, and pink also look good, perhaps with a cream color on the outside. The colors and patterns of sunny Provence have always been distinctive—rather than just white, furniture and walls are often painted in soft creams, light greens, and cooling blues.

ABOVE & RIGHT
Old painted beams given a wash of off-white or putty colored paint help integrate new wooden railings with the rest of the house. Many people are afraid to paint beams but farmhouses all over Europe would have been lime-washed annually as part of a general spring clean. It not only makes small spaces seem larger but also ensures walls are not divided by oppressive dark lines. Beams can be painted in solid colors or by giving them a light wash, depending on their tone and whether you want any of the wood grain to show through.

An English Chippendale style chair has been given the French treatment. Painted in gray over deep blue, it has then been lightly distressed. Its seat has been covered in some old French linen. Next to it, a French buffet has been painted in the same gray. The moldings have been picked out in white while its top is a graphite black to match the urn and drawer handle. All the paintwork has been waxed.

Parisian

So many artists and designers have lived in Paris that it is not surprising the city has developed its own style of living and decor. Jeanne Lanvin was just one fashion designer to make her mark, and a recreation of her blue-embroidered, silk-lined living room is on view at the Musée des Arts Décoratifs in Paris.

COCO'S LASTING INFLUENCE

However, probably the most important influences for elegant, chic style comes from Gabrielle "Coco" Chanel, whose apartment has come to epitomize the design extravagance of the Parisians.

Unlike her fashion style, which was uncluttered and tailored, her apartment was very theatrical. One high-ceilinged room had shelves of leather-bound books, walls painted a pale celadon green, two large mirrors, and a wide, rectangular sofa covered in fawn-colored suede.

It was, though, the objects in this private sitting room that made the place so extraordinary and baroque in expression. Several came in pairs, such as two life-sized black deer that grazed in one corner, two very large oriental coromandel screens that flanked the fireplace, and, at the entrance to the room, two large, gilded blackamoors who held torches high. Either side of the fireplace two tall, gilded art deco carvings of figures and drapery made an eye-catching feature.

COMBINING RURAL MOTIFS

In contrast to these grand statements, Coco Chanel loved the simple countryside image of ears of wheat, as shown in a round, glass-topped table with a gilded metal wheatsheaf as the base. By its side, a big vase was often filled with real wheat, while on the wall hung an image of a gilded wheat ear by Salvador Dali.

The room was also furnished with a beautifully painted bureau and an ornate gilded console table. Above all this hung a huge crystal chandelier. This is the Paris of the grand gesture. It is not an easy style to achieve and

ABOVE
This beautiful 1950s screen is painted in a style influenced by Chinoiserie. The screen is a great device for giving a theaterlike ambience to a room. The table with its shapely cabriole legs has been painted, leaving the central leather top uncluttered.

LEFT
Black with turquoise blue and touches of red make an edgy combination. As the eye travels from one item to the next it carries a color to connect them. Here, the painting is the key because it contains all the colors on the mantelpiece.

Above Left & Right

The red of the buttons and the curtain fabric are picked up in the rest of the room in small ways. The pillow on the bergere chair has an inset that is made from the same black and white toile design as the curtains, and set into plain red with borders of a spotted fabric that matches the line on the drape.

requires at least one piece of decoration that is special. The high street is not the place to look, but for those who enjoy browsing in markets and who can see how something unusual might work, this challenging style may be just right.

Haute Couture Additions

Coco Chanel's clothes have inspired Parisian interior design as much, if not more than, her eye for unique decoration. The neat, clean elegance of her famous black and white tailored jacket can be adapted for curtains and pillows. As well as this, *haute couture* in fifties and sixties Paris used large and interesting buttons on jackets and

coats. These are a wonderful way to add decoration to curtains, pillows, and lampshades.

Bohemian Style

The other predominant style from Paris is inspired by the artists who made the city their home and can be explained by looking at their paintings. The art scene has largely deserted Paris these days but, particularly before the Second World War, the city was a hive of intellectual and artistic activity, the home of dada and surrealism.

The Paris style of the bohemian is inventive—turning mannequins into lamps or using them for some other form of decoration is a note straight out of the surrealists' book.

unlined linen curtains with braid

Unbleached linen with an ecclesiastical braid along the leading edge makes a simple but practical curtain in a study. The linen is fairly heavy but has quite an open weave so it offers protection from bright sun while allowing a little light to enter the room. Use a braid that matches the style of the room—it could be vintage or modern. So that no hem is visible, the fabric is folded to the front and the braid is sewn over the top to cover it.

1 Cut out the fabric for the curtains to fit the window. Hem the top and bottom conventionally or leave the edges unworked if the braid is to cover the top, sides, and bottom. Fold over the edges to be braided into a hem and iron flat. The hem, which should face into the room, should be small enough for the chosen braid to cover.

2 Pin the braid on to the linen in line with the edge. If you are having to turn corners, miter them by folding the braid in on one side.

3 Tack the braid on to the linen with cotton thread and remove the pins. Using cotton thread that matches the color of the chosen braid, sew neatly down the length of the braid on both sides so that it is well secured.

crackle varnished console table

Crackle varnish is a technique that copies the look of old varnish, which, over time, has cracked like the surface of an old master painting. In previous centuries, finely painted furniture, perhaps decorated with flowers or découpage, would have been varnished. Over the years the varnish cracks due to movement in the wood or temperature changes. On an original piece of old furniture these cracks would not cover the furniture but would be seen perhaps on a drawer front or part of a table top and they would be uneven. Today, we see this crackling of varnish on furniture as a decoration in itself. Although a rural look, this is one that originated in the château. The technique is carried out in two stages using a water based proprietary kit, and is best done on flat areas rather than carving or molding.

YOU WILL NEED
Fine sandpaper
500 ml Old White
Chalk Paint
Crackle varnish kit
3 large paintbrushes
Hairdryer
100 ml dark wax
100 ml clear wax
Dry cotton cloth

FAR LEFT
A modern console table with simplified cabriole legs has been given the château look by crackling the top only, and applying brass leaf to the molding. The remainder of the table has been given a gently distressed paint effect (see page 107). The first layer was Louis Blue, which can be seen inside the drawer, then Old White was painted over the top before distressing.

crackle varnished console table

1 To prepare the piece, rub with fine sandpaper to make the surface smooth, then apply two coats of Old White paint. Apply the first part of the kit over the main flat surfaces. Allow to dry. You can assist this process by using a hairdryer. For finer cracks, apply the liquid thinly, altering the thickness to give variation. It does not matter in which direction the brush strokes are applied.

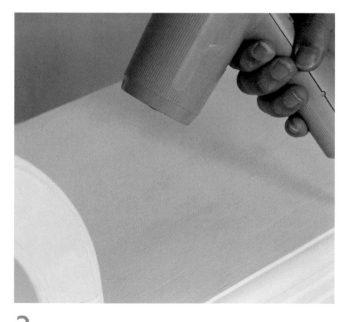

2 Apply the second part of the kit. In the pot, this is a viscous liquid but it is easy to spread. Paint it all over the area to which you have applied the first part of the kit. Treat each area separately. As both parts of the kit are the same color, it can be difficult to see if the surface is completely covered, so tilt the furniture in the light to find any areas you may have missed. Vary the thickness of the application but take care not to make it too thick, or the result may end up looking like liquid puddles rather than cracks. Layers applied to vertical surfaces may drip.

3 For the cracks to appear, the surface needs to be heated. This can be done artificially by using a hairdryer, or it can be done by leaving the furniture in a warm atmosphere, either a heated or sun-warmed room. The cracks may take from five minutes to half an hour to appear and will at first be seen at certain angles only.

4 To make the cracks more visible, apply dark wax over all the surfaces, making certain you brush it in all directions so that it penetrates deep into the cracks. It may look messy at this stage but don't panic. Don't let the dark wax dry out as it will be difficult to remove.

5 Wipe off the excess dark wax using a clean cotton cloth, rubbing into the cracks as you go, making certain that they are all filled. You should be able to clean off a large amount of the wax.

alternative uses

Use crackle varnish on any small, flat area of furniture such as a stool top, panel, or plain frame. As it uses transparent varnish it also works well over découpage and stenciling.

6 Wipe some clear wax lightly over the surface. The aim is for the surface to be as clean as you can make it with the dark wax remaining in the cracks.

lining walls with fabric

You Will Need

Lengths of fabric

Scissors

Staple gun

Length of braid

Fabric adhesive

Lining walls with fabric instantly makes a room soft and calm, whether using formal *toiles de jouy*—as in the living room opposite—or a finely woven linen, which would suit a cottage room. The ambience is also improved as the fabric absorbs sound and covers any blemishes. Sew lengths of single-width fabric together into panels or simply overlap them and iron flat.

2 Position the second length of fabric so that it slightly overlaps the first. Staple it then pull it tight and fix at the bottom. Pull it taut enough so there is no need to fix the fabric down the overlapping sides.

1 Cut the fabric into the length you need for the wall—overestimate as you can always cut off the excess. Hold the fabric so it aligns down a door post, and staple it to the wall halfway along the top to establish a firm connection. Pull the fabric down towards the floor, making certain to keep it straight and taut, and staple in the center, at the bottom, and on both sides. Return to the top, pulling the fabric again so it stretches, and work from the center outwards, stapling as you go along the top and then down the outer edges.

3 Choose a braid or ribbon to glue lightly around the outer edges of the fabric panels. Here a light herringbone tape has been used to cover the unsightly staples.

antiqued cherub

A very beautiful 18th century wooden cherub standing on a pedestal graces this entrance hall, its wood bleached almost white with age and its paintwork distressed and flaking. Pieces like this are rare but you can achieve something similar using an ordinary stone statue from a garden center— this one is several years old so already has a bit of patina.

1 Paint the statue in places with Old White paint using the edge of the brush to go over the raised areas rather than pushing the paint into the recesses. This will bring out the design and shapes of the statue. Apply a little at first, then add more as you become more confident about the way you want the statue to look.

YOU WILL NEED
100 ml Old White
Chalk Paint
Medium paintbrush
Dry dirt
Soft brush

2 Using some earth from a pot plant (it is likely to be clean and light) rub it into parts of the wet paint and into the recesses. It will mix with the white paint to make it a little dirty and grayed, knocking back the white highlights such as on the rounded tummy and cheeks so that they don't appear to stick out too much. Also darken some of the crevices with the dirt.

3 When the statue is dry, get rid of any excess dirt by dusting it with a soft dry brush.

painting an old gilded mirror frame

This old frame had been painted with a gold colored paint that made it look rather flat and cheap. The design of the molding is the classical acanthus, making it perfect for transforming into a French-style mirror frame. Gold showing through white suits the genteel look of the country *manoir* so, to achieve a similar look, find frames with pronounced carving. The technique could be adapted to suit any look by choosing the right colors.

YOU WILL NEED

100 ml Old White Chalk Paint

Medium paintbrush

Paper towel, cloth or sponge

2 Using a damp paper towel, cloth or sponge, wipe over the raised carving, leaving paint in the recesses. By wiping just a few times, paint can be left as a wash over some of the raised areas so the effect is soft, or it can be wiped quite cleanly so the difference in the gold and white is strongly contrasted. Work over the whole frame so the effect is even. Allow to dry. Then put a mirror in the frame, or choose a picture for it.

1 Apply the soft chalk paint over the frame, making certain it goes into all the recesses. Allow it to dry thoroughly.

3 An alternative method of achieving this look is to pass a flat brush of dryish paint lightly over the raised molding. The effect leaves more gilding than paint, and may suit a different room or picture.

provençal *armoire*
with cicada fabric

This is a new *armoire* from the south of France, near the Spanish border. It was first painted entirely in gray, then with Duck Egg Blue and Celadon Green, with Louis Blue on the inside of the cupboard and on the drawer fronts. Finally, it was distressed all over using clear and dark wax and sandpaper. The textured painting, especially on the top carved area, is emphasized with the use of dark wax rubbed into crevices. Like many *armoires*, this one has doors that can be either glazed or covered in fabric—here the voile chosen has an embroidered cicada design, the cicada being a popular motif in Provence.

YOU WILL NEED
Length of fabric (voile)
Needle and cotton
Sewing machine (optional)
Dowling
Bradawl
Eyelet screws

LEFT & RIGHT
The French often hang a voile fabric in cabinet doors instead of glass, because the fabric allows air through but keeps out insects. This cabinet has been made using my own part linen, part cotton voile with embroidered cicadas.

provençal armoire with cicada fabric

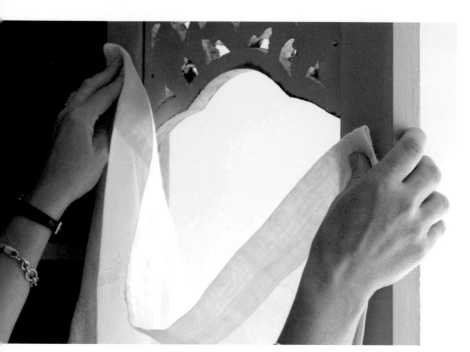

2 Mark with a pencil where the eyelet screws must go, then use a bradawl to make holes in the wood.

1 To give the fabric the right gathered look, use a piece half as wide again as the opening it will cover. Hem the fabric around all the edges by turning under 1 in. (2.5 cm), turning under again and stitching. At the top, fold over 3 in. (8 cm), stitching along the folded edge. Stitch again about 1 in. (2.5 cm) above this stitching line. The gap between the lines of stitching should be wide enough to inset your length of dowling.

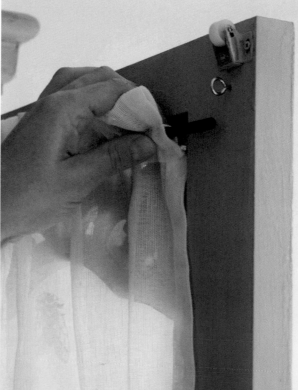

3 Secure the eyelet screws. Put up the curtain by pushing the dowling through the eyelets. Pull down the curtain gently until it is fairly taut and hanging as you want it.

alternative uses

Use the same idea on a glazed door or window. Thin cottons in faded stripes or vintage linens give a more rustic look while brightly colored fabrics evoke the Riviera.

softly tailored curtains

For these curtains my inspiration came from the *haute couture*, and in particular Chanel, jackets of the 1950s—a soft yet tailored design classic. Instead of using the characteristic braiding on the leading edge, I have used two other devices from dressmaking—a different colored thread that emphasizes the hems around the curtain, and large vintage French buttons, sewn on at intervals. For the top of the curtain, or heading, the turnover is big enough to look like a collar or cuff. Instead of a gathered heading, I wanted to be able to draw the curtains so that they pull out to resemble a panel. I therefore decided against a traditional curtain tape and have used buckram, which keeps the heading upright and firm. The curtains have been made with my own heavyweight creamy white pure Manoir Blanc linen, then lined with a red spotty fabric, just like a jacket.

YOU WILL NEED

Annie Sloane's Manoir Blanc linen cut to length

Buckram cut to length

Needle and cotton in contrasting color

Sewing machine

Buttons and same color thread

Hook pins

LEFT & RIGHT
The curtains have been hung on an old brass pole. The weight of the linen helps to give softness to the tailored design so the folds are not too stiff and rigid. By using strong fine cotton, the curtains could be more formal looking. Set against the muted tone of the taupe wall with a neo-classical mirror, a purple pitcher and Château Grey paintwork on the table and lamp base, the red and amber buttons are bright and clear.

softly tailored curtains

1 Decide how big you want the heading to be—I decided on about one-eighteenth of the total drop but you could make it even larger. Place the buckram into the heading, as shown, fold and iron the sides.

alternative uses

Add braid instead of buttons along the edge of the folded hem or make a hemmed edging at the bottom of Roman blinds, adding buttons too. Give pillows the tailored look with buttons and edging.

2 Open out the heading and, on the right side, pin the buckram into place by folding over the top and side hems. Tack in place then overstitch along the sides of the curtain using brown thread. If hand stitching, use thicker cotton and larger stitches.

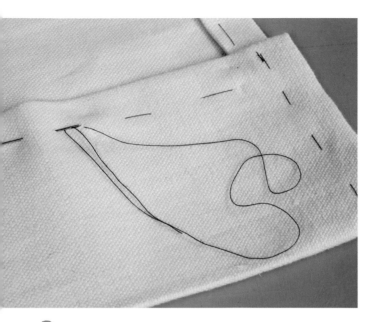

3 Fold over the fabric along over the front of the curtain, iron flat, then pin and tack as shown. (If you are going to line the curtains, this is when to do it.) Machine stitch around the heading to help keep it stiff and firm.

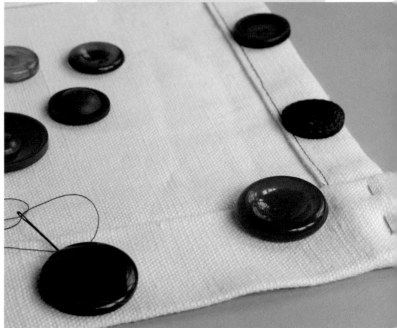

4 At the base of the curtain, fold the hem around to the front, pin and tack. Overstitch as before using machine or hand stitching. Choose a selection of buttons varying in shape, pattern, and size to go down the sides and even along the bottom. Measure out and mark their positions with pins. Sew the buttons on using the same color thread as the buttons. Take care to conceal the knot in the fabric so nothing can be seen on the reverse.

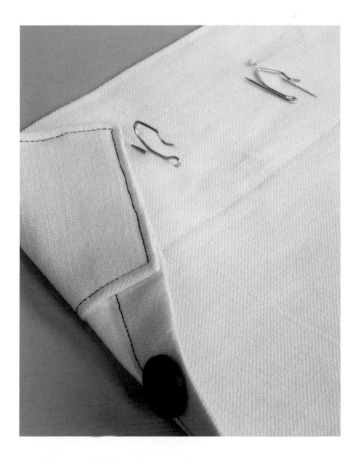

5 Measure the width of the curtain and mark with a pin where the curtain hook pins should be placed. Make sure the hook pins are attached so the curtains will hang properly and straight. They may need adjusting because your floor may not be even.

painted
bureau

YOU WILL NEED

500 ml paint in two similar tones
Old White Chalk Paint
Small square paintbrush
Pencil (optional)
Large paintbrush
500 ml clear wax
500 ml dark wax
Cloth

This oak desk, probably from the 1940s, looked heavy and dark, and was without shape or grace in its natural state. However, being a useful size, I decide to paint it and bring out its boxlike qualities using colors inspired by Coco Chanel's famous jackets. An inset border around the drawers called for a contrasting color, like braid on a jacket.

LEFT & BELOW

The bureau has a been given a Parisian look, making it a fitting partner for the old French mannequin from the turn of the last century, which has been covered in newspaper and adapted into a lamp base. The outside of the bureau has been painted in a combination of deep lilac and dark blue. These have mixed and merged so that the change of color resembles the patina of age. Around the drawers, the inset border has been painted an off-white to give an extra feature.

1 Choose two colors that are near each other on the color wheel, such as the deep lilac and warm dark blue used here. While the first coat was still wet, the next color was applied, working it into the wet paint so there is no apparent line. Paint the front of the furniture at the same time, so that the drawers do not stand out from the frame when they are closed.

painted bureau

Like a silk lining in a jacket, the inside of this bureau has been painted in a stunning red called Red Beret. To give variation, the red has been darkened in places with a little Burgundian Red, then waxed thoroughly.

2 With white paint and a small square brush, paint around the edge of the drawers. If there is no border, draw one with a pencil then fill it in.

3 Use a big brush to apply first clear then dark wax. Work both of them all over the surface, leaving fairly clear areas as well as dark ones. Try to make these areas merge so there are no obvious patches.

4 Wipe off the excess with a clean cloth. Polish the bureau the next day so that the paintwork develops a slight shine.

chapter 2

Kitchen & Dining Room

Although this is a cottage kitchen with beams, it looks for inspiration to the salon rather than the scullery. A large painting of plants and a garden wall turns a relatively basic kitchen into a stylish one, particularly with the addition of the lampshades and urn of hydrangeas.

Château

The kitchen of the true French château is likely to have been a large, basic affair with spacious cupboards for all the china and silverware, copper pans, and a large cooking range. In style it would have been based on the kitchen of a country house. Nowadays, a big kitchen has become the room where the whole family spends time and, as its use has changed, so has its look. A country kitchen is not always appropriate in urban areas, so the ever-popular château style has been reintroduced into the kitchen with chandeliers, gold-colored fittings, marble, and comfort.

Gilding in the kitchen is a new idea, but if the room is used daily for entertainment and relaxation, why not give it a touch of glamour? Find paintings for the walls, too. Kitchens nowadays are clean and not steam filled or full of frying fat, so having relatively delicate items, such as paintings, is not out of the question any more. Go for gold!

GLITTERING SOPHISTICATION

The elegance and sophistication of the château dining room has always been a style to aspire to. Its classic image is that of a sumptuous dining table laid with a crisp white linen tablecloth and napkins, silverware, goblets, and wine glasses, all set out under a central, sparkling chandelier.

This look is not so hard to achieve. Instead of a tablecloth an old table can be painted, transforming a dark object into something light and bright and, of course, very French looking. Remember the French are not afraid to paint wood unless the wood is very special indeed. If you use the right paint, no primers are needed, so painting a large object such as a table need not take days. Start after breakfast and you should be able to eat on it in time for dinner that night.

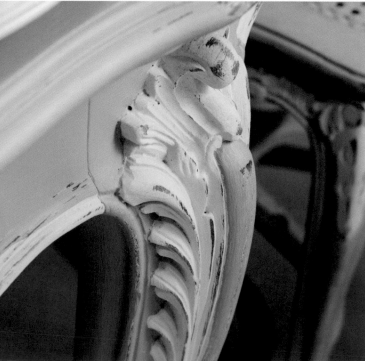

ABOVE LEFT & LEFT
White china, bone-handled silverware, and linen napkins are very chic. The carved details of the table are painted in white, the rest of the table in gray. Distressing lifts the color, showing a little of the warm wood beneath. Clear wax gives a durable finish that has the soft, mellow look of the original.

ABOVE
Glasses with a frosted monogram, such as these, complement the look, as do elegant vintage carafes and decanters, so look out for these as well.

RIGHT
Keeping colors to a minimum and with a huge crystal chandelier suspended over the delightfully painted dining table, the scene is set for understated luxury, especially with the magnificent old carved armoire in the background. The typically French chairs have carved flowers on their frames and caned backs. Chairs such as this often have a padded seat.

Country

The country kitchen and dining room are, of course, much less grand than the château's, but some elements are the same. The style of the French country kitchen is much sought after these days because it is a symbol of everything we hold dear, and the opposite of our usual everyday environment—there is no plastic, no shiny metal, no harsh lighting. The kitchen has a preponderance of wood, and is usually painted. It has baskets for storage, stone or wood flooring and the lighting is task orientated. It is essentially a combination of kitchen and living room where everything is done from preparing, cooking, and eating food, to gathering around the table at the end of the day. We do not all live in houses that can accommodate this but the basic principles of the French country kitchen are still desirable.

Ubiquitous *Armoire*

Every country manor house had at least one *armoire* and more often two, one in the kitchen and one in the dining room. The kitchen *armoire* would hold everyday, practical utensils while the one in the dining room would be used for the prettier pieces, kept for special occasions, holidays, and Sundays.

Although simply the French version of a cupboard, the *armoire* is not only elegant but also very practical. Many *armoires* are entirely portable, coming apart into several pieces—the back, sides, doors, base, and decorative *chapeau*, which is always the last piece to be put on as it keeps everything in place. A clever, serrated fixing system allows there to be as many shelves as are needed and for changes to be made easily. Sometimes called marriage *armoires*, they were part of the bride's dowry and were taken by her to her new home, often filled with linen.

Armoires were made by local carpenters in the local style, which varied tremendously from region to region, but the owner of a country manor house might well aspire to having *armoires* like those in the château. There the design had a direct link to furniture originally made for the great châteaux, such as Versailles.

ABOVE
The shelf for beans and herbs in glass jars has been painted in gray and the lovely shape is emphasized by painting the edges in white. Collecting interesting pitchers or tureens in cream, white or gray adds color and interest to a room. The copper pots hang from simple dark red painted hooks, making a big statement in the room.

RIGHT
The sink gilded candlesticks stand beside large terra cotta pots. The plate rack under the shelf has been bricked in and then covered in stone tiles, leaving a little alcove for soap and scourers. VIntage French sinks are often shallow but this is a new one in the old style.

RUSTIC STYLE

As the hub of the house, the rustic kitchen feels very comfortable and welcoming. This is not the look of the fitted kitchen with neat lines and uniformity. Avoid using conventional wall cabinets unless they can be painted—a row of fitted cabinets will destroy the look of an old-fashioned kitchen immediately. A kitchen range with a number of freestanding cupboards fit the style much better. Have an *armoire* for china and even food, a porcelain sink and wooden work surfaces. Use baskets for storage and have open shelves, or hide unsightly pots and pans with a gingham curtain. If you have room, find a good solid shapely

old table. Paint its legs and leave the top bare so that it can be scrubbed clean. A large table is usually the focal point of the French country kitchen, where food is prepared and eaten, with no recourse to a formal dining room.

MIXING OLD AND NEW

The trick is to unify your old and new furniture by painting the pieces. Paint them all slightly differently but make sure they work well together. Use whites, creams, and perhaps a muddy blue, and you can paint the back of open shelves in a shade picked out from, say, red gingham curtains. Display white and cream pitchers and bowls on open shelves.

ABOVE

This delightful armoire *with turned pilasters has been painted in gray, distressed to reveal the wood in places, and also in a red color like that used for priming originally. Inside the glazed doors the interior has been painted in the same Scandinavian Pink.*

LEFT

Dramatically shaped legs adorn this fine table. The linen tablecloth is, in fact, a wringer cloth, which was originally used to protect very fine linen as it was wound through the drums of a wringer.

ABOVE
A basket of white linen dish towels or torchons with red embroidered monograms sits in front of a set of large wooden chopping blocks.

BELOW
Fancy escutcheons (door furniture) are typical of French doors. Some, such as this one, are long and ornate. Although they may be polished, many are too old and tarnished to clean properly. The decorative painted egg is from the Ukraine.

ABOVE
A set of four drawers, painted in rich ox blood red, is perfect for kitchen spices. It sits on the gray and white, painted and distressed mantelpiece, set off by a simple pitcher of parsley.

In the rustic kitchen pride of place is reserved for a locally made *armoire*. Those from Brittany are usually heavily carved with abstract patterns and lozenge shapes while in the south the design tends to be curvier and lightly carved. An original *armoire* will be very expensive but a reproduction in pine will look excellent when painted.

The seating around the table is more likely to be made up of benches than individual chairs because in this way more people could be accommodated for large family meals. If you prefer individual chairs, find ones with rush seats if possible, and paint them. Floors in the country style kitchen are likely to be of stone or terra cotta tiles but wooden floors are also common. Walls should be uneven so, if yours are rather too perfect, give them an uneven wash of slightly thinned-down matt paint. Tile around the sink area only. The main point to remember when creating a rustic kitchen is to keep things simple.

Provençal

In a true Provençal kitchen the textures are rough, natural, and earthy, much white is used and there is an even greater emphasis on simplicity than in the rest of France.

The French understand simplicity. In many hands "simple" can mean plain, dull or uncomfortable. A simple French country interior, however, has the same approach as the best of French food—few but good ingredients. Each ingredient of the Provençal kitchen is carefully chosen so it is not only practical but fits well in the space. The shapes in the room are made up of the turn of a chair back or the *chapeau* on the *armoire*.

The basic canvas is made up of chalky ocher or white-washed walls and stone or terra cotta tiled floors. In the south, tiles are plentiful, perhaps influenced by the Mediterranean and the closeness of Spain and Morocco. On the floor you might also find red and yellow ocher stone but on the walls and work surfaces you will certainly find color—yellow ochers, earthy green and strong blue are favored. On the Riviera, Italian marble is often used for splashbacks and floors.

SOFTNESS AND COLOR

Look for softly painted furniture with curves, stone or porcelain sinks, light curtaining, and old-fashioned cooking pots to enhance the look. In a Provençal kitchen, earthenware pottery in the shape of large platters, pitchers, bowls, and *marmites*—a cooking pot with lid and handles—are all displayed. The furniture is likely to be freestanding, as in all country kitchens, and all painted.

Provençal dining chairs are particularly lovely. They have curvy ladder backs with rush seating and many are painted in two colors to display the carving. Green the color of basil, a dusky blue, and yellow ocher are the colors that work best for the paintwork. The motif of a basket of flowers is common on the backs of chairs. Tables often have painted legs but, in the kitchen, the top is left as plain wood. In the dining room, if a tablecloth isn't being used, the table looks best painted.

LEFT & ABOVE
An old kitchen shelf with three good drawers leant itself to being painted in stunning Provençal colors—Old White chalk paint picked out in Red Beret and Chateau Grey. Red was used on the molding, the inside of the decorative trim and in the groove of the back paneling before the green gray was painted over the back, the molding and the drawer fronts. The whole piece was waxed, then the drawers were painted red and rubbed back so the texture on them is a little coarser. Finally, the piece was gently distressed and waxed again.

Along the coast the bright sunshine of the long summer months demands stronger colors. Tomato red, bright sea blue, light olive green, and sunflower yellow all look good. Colorful striped fabrics look great for curtains and pillows in kitchens and dining areas. This is a more contemporary French look but it works well combined with old painted pieces.

Parisian

ABOVE
All sorts of silverware are useful for Parisian style. Here a drawer is filled with cutlery that has been collected over the years from auctions and markets.

ABOVE RIGHT
In this modish dining room, inspired by frequent visits to Paris and an interest in haute couture, the imaginative color scheme is topped off by a wonderfully irreverent set of pictures. The colors are centered around the warm, Scandinavian Pink used on the walls. Dusky Melon is used inside the cupboard and picked up in the paintings, while the rest of the room is finished in neutral blacks, grays, and off-white. The table has been painted, distressed and waxed with Graphite Black on top and Paris Grey over the pink on the legs. Overhead, two candles in hanging glass lanterns give a lovely central light, perfect for dining.

The Parisian dining room may be incorporated in the kitchen or separate, and may emulate the understated elegance of the château or show bohemian flair. In any case, it is definitely chic, and needs to be a little outrageous to entertain the eye.

ECLECTIC TRADITIONS
Although Parisians feel at liberty to take ideas from all parts of France and from any period of history, the Parisian dining room or kitchen is unlikely to be country style. The look will show discernment, mixing old flea-market finds with swish new pieces. The discreet charm of French retro is particularly appealing. The photographs of Paris by Henri Cartier-Bresson and especially Robert Doisneau—his "Kiss by the Hotel de Ville" is iconic—

evoke the style and magic of Paris in the 1950s. Old black and white photography from this period gives a special contrast and makes a great statement for a dining room.

Use witty, perhaps even ironic, touches by adding red gingham, the archetypal French fabric. The look of the slightly dark French bistro with white lace at the window and red gingham tablecloths could be a lovely way to decorate a Parisian dining room, recalling the traditional look.

A strong color on the walls, a black table top and a mass of pictures are all ways to help develop the drama inherent in this style. Lighting is also vital in the dining area because it creates such atmosphere. Characteristic French lighting could vary from an ornate glass chandelier or a smaller brass one. Paint brass if it seems too shiny and bright.

ABOVE

A buffet, the French version of a sideboard, painted in Country Grey might be a cupboard with drawers and doors, or else include a top like a dresser to be used for china or food. This one has been painted and distressed and decorated with a china ram's head.

RIGHT

This clever lampshade made from a shiny colander allows the light to shine through the silvery metal holes to give a stylish, modern look.

ruffled slip-over pillow cover

Using a soft fabric to make a loosely hanging ruffle, create a stylish pillow cover to enclose a simple foam pillow form. Ruffled pillow covers, made from simple fabrics such as light and bright checked cottons, are a great way to bring style and comfort to a kitchen.

1 Cut two squares of fabric to make the pillow cover, each the size of the pillow form plus 4 in. (10 cm). Fold 2 in. (5 cm) over and tack in place.

2 To make the ruffle, or skirt, cut a piece of fabric measuring double the length of three sides of the seat (the back of the chair has no ruffle) by the desired drop from the chair seat plus 1 in. (2.5 cm). Fold over 1 in. (2.5 cm) and iron the fabric along one length and both edges. Machine sew the hem and the sides of the skirt.

3 Pleat the skirt, pinning and tacking it in place around three sides of one fabric square, wrong sides facing. Machine stitch it in place.

4 Sew a zipper along the fourth side of the fabric square, then sew its other side on to the second square of fabric. Turn the right sides of the fabric together and machine stitch the pillow together, adding ribbon ties on the back before turning right sides out.

neo-classical gilded table

YOU WILL NEED

1 liter Paris Grey
Chalk Paint

2 large paintbrushes

Pencil

100 ml gold size

Book of brass leaf

500 ml clear wax

Fine sandpaper

250 ml dark wax

Cotton cloth

I have been able to use an unfashionable, highly polished reproduction table because all the dark and shiny wood will be hidden by paint and brass gilding. Although the table is in English Regency style, its new look ensures it can work well in an individualistic interior as long as complete authenticity is not required. The look is distressed gold but the effect is achieved with brass leaf, and the technique is finished with wax, which is soft, mellow, and very strong.

FAR LEFT & ABOVE
The gilded table sits at the center of a room that is a marvelous mix of neo-classical and Parisian couture styles. The main thrust of the room is neo-classical with the large marbled obelisk and urn set in front of the wonderful green of the wall, inspired by the Louis XVI apartment at the palace of Fontainebleau. The matching curtains are made from very soft, fine silk and cotton voile, and were designed for the owner by Christian Dior. The white cockatoo peeking out from behind the urn shows an appealing quirkiness. On the floor a magnificent needlepoint Berlin rug, like a rather bold Aubusson, is a fine match for the strong wall color.

1 Cover the table with Chalk Paint because this adheres to anything and so the surface does not need to be prepared and primed. I chose an elegant Paris Grey that contrasts well with gold. Paint the whole table using smooth all-direction strokes. Apply two coats for a good finish.

neo-classical gilded table

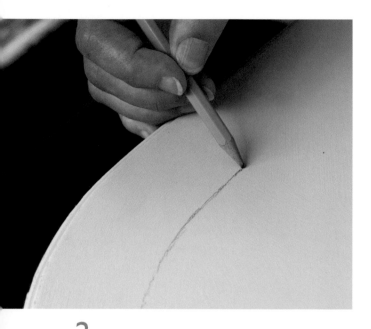

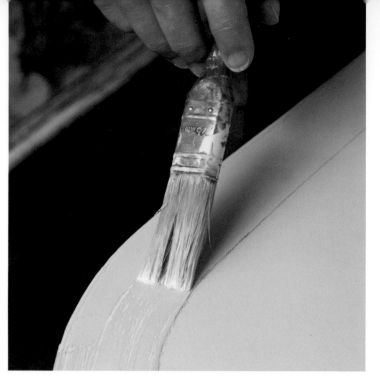

3 Apply gold size (water based adhesive for metallic leaf) to the outlined area and to the raised molded edge of the table. The size dries quickly so don't let it get sticky and thick. At first the adhesive is white but, as it dries, it becomes quite transparent. This takes several minutes, especially when it is applied to an absorbent surface.

2 For a rim of gold around the edge of the table, first mark out the band to be gilded. I used a pencil for this, steadying my hand with my little and next fingers along the table's edge. Don't work too quickly and try to draw a continuous line.

4 The size is ready for the brass leaf when it is transparent. It will remain sticky for several months, so you do not need to hurry. Each sheet of leaf is 5 in. (12.5 cm) square. Holding the sheet in one hand and a soft brush in the other, partly allow it to drop and partly guide it on to the size with the brush.

5 Brush the excess away. The leaf will not fix anywhere there is no size. I deliberately left the recessed part of the molded edges unsized so the brass would remain on the raised areas only.

6   Brass leaf needs to be sealed so that it will not tarnish. Clear wax is a good sealer because it helps to dull the brass and allows it to be distressed. Apply a soft clear wax with a brush.

7   To distress the leaf, use very fine sandpaper. Rub gently all over the leaf so that some of the gray background shows through. Don't rub it evenly but leave some areas free from distressing.

8   To give the final antiquing, use a dark wax all over. At first this looks very dark. Apply with a brush and remove the excess with a cloth. Work in small areas rather than all over the table.

alternative

All sorts of variations are possible with a table such as this. For instance, make a central oval or more than one band around the outside. To make it even more unusual, you could stencil a laurel border around the outside of the table in place of the gilding.

9   Finish off with a layer of clear wax, which will remove more of the dark wax, but leave it where you want the table to be darker. The molding should be filled with wax. The next day, polish the table to give it a sheen.

armoire with stenciled doors

The idea of the stencil is to make a random all-over pattern that resembles damask, or the type of fabric that used to be pinned inside the door as decoration in the old days. The *armoire* should be painted in neutral colors on the outside so that when it is opened it reveals a gloriously colored interior, set off by the stenciled door. The idea of painting *armoires* is an old one, particularly favored in the châteaux of Provence and mountain areas. Many reproduction and vintage pieces can be given a new lease of life with colored interiors and stenciled doors. Large and small flowers, as well as damask patterns, are ideal stencil designs.

YOU WILL NEED

Old White Chalk Paint (optional)

Large paintbrush

100 ml of two shades of paint—
Old Ochre and Country Grey

Roller tray and roller

Stencil (acetate)

100 ml clear wax

50 ml dark wax

Cotton cloth

LEFT & RIGHT

An oak-leaf stencil pattern has been applied in a loose and random way over the inside of the door of this old French armoire, *which is used to store plates and glassware. By using the same cream and putty gray colors for stenciling as have been painted on the outside of the* armoire, *the piece looks a cohesive unit. The inside has been painted in Scandinavian Pink over Cream and waxed with clear and some dark wax for depth. Finally, it was distressed to reveal the dark color of the old wood.*

armoire with stenciled doors

1   The interior of many *armoires*, including the doors, will have been painted already and possibly waxed. If this is the case with yours, the first thing to do is to give them two coats of white paint—the idea is to keep the inside of the doors light and patterned. Keep the paint a little dry and brush in all directions rather than just up and down. This ensures that the surface is textured with obvious brush marks.

2   Pour your two chosen colors into a roller tray, keeping them separate. They should be either different tones of similar colors or different colors of similar tones. Roll the sponge roller in the tray, so that it takes up the two colors, but try not to overload it so that it is sodden through. A little paint goes a long way.

3   Hold the stencil to the door and push the roller over it. The whole trick about this stenciling method is not to have an obvious repeat pattern. So change direction, overlap the patterns and take care not to make it too even. Move the stencil randomly.

4 When the paint is dry, brush clear wax all over, making certain everything is covered.

5 The next step is rather alarming as you will feel you are almost obliterating all your careful work by covering it in dark wax. Don't panic and take heart. Brush the wax into all the crevices of the paintwork.

6 Take a cotton cloth and wipe off as much of the excess wax as you can, working it into the paintwork as you go. This will allow you to see more of the stencil design again.

7 Now brush clear wax quite lightly over the surface to remove the dark wax, while keeping traces of it in the grooves of the brush marks, so the surface looks clean but the brush marks are pronounced. Clean off some areas more than others to achieve the varied patina effect that gives a piece of furniture depth. Use a cloth to wipe off the excess and then polish the surface.

three-color printed floor

YOU WILL NEED
Roller tray and roller
Masking tape and string
1 liter Paris Grey Chalk Paint
for base
250 ml each of two other
colored paints—Old
White and Cream
Sponge, square-shaped
Large paintbrush
1 liter clear, extra strong
varnish

The pattern of an old tiled floor may be re-created in any number of colors, giving a concrete floor an unusual and interesting look. I have chosen a rustic feel, using gray and buttery yellow with white. Painted and then varnished the floor is very strong and will withstand a lot of wear.

2   Go over some of the squares you have already done with a third color. Do some next to each other and leave gaps in other areas. The sponge will cover the squares unevenly so some of the white will show but it is this randomness that looks so appealing.

1   Use a roller to cover the floor with the base gray color. Starting in the center of the room, tape a piece of string to the floor from one side of the room to the other. Spread white paint evenly in the roller tray, dip the square sponge into it, making sure it is wholly covered, and press onto the floor at regular intervals, using the string as a guide. Repeat on the other side of the string. When you have done two lines of squares, move the string for the next two lines and continue until the whole room is done.

3   Give the floor two coats of extra strong varnish, using a brush at the edges and a roller over the rest.

stained and varnished furniture

This technique is best for new wood so the paint is absorbed completely, leaving the grain visible. Choose a wood that can be enhanced by the paint color—tulip wood, with its interesting grain, is ideal. Here, neither the ladder-backed chairs nor the pine cupboard have knots on the outside, so no sap will bleed through.

You will need

Unsealed wooden furniture

100 ml Chalk Paint

Large paintbrush

Sponge and water

100 ml clear water based varnish

1 Apply a soft, water soluble paint to the surface in a loose way, taking care not to cover the whole surface. When using the very chalkiest toned paints, allow the paint to dry, but if the color is strong you may need to start the second stage while it is still wet. In this case, tackle one side at a time.

2 With a sponge and some water start wiping off the paint, wringing out the excess in clean water. Take off as much paint as you need to achieve the color you want but try not to get the wood too soaked because this opens up the grain and can make it "fray," especially if the furniture is pine.

3 Allow the paint to dry completely. Then, using a brush, apply water based varnish evenly all over.

stylish buttoned napkins

Napkins in personalized designs are popular in French homes. I have made these sharp and showy napkins in the same fabric, then given each a distinctive button. Napkins are easy to make and are good to give as gifts. Make yours stylish and original, using scraps of left-over cotton or linen.

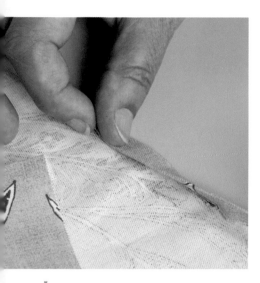

1 Cut out a square of fabric the size you want your napkin to be, allowing 2 in. (5 cm) all round for the hem. Fold over the edges twice, as shown, and iron flat.

2 When you get to a corner, fold in the two edges as before and secure with a pin. Using a pair of sharp scissors, cut off the excess fabric to avoid the corner being too bulky.

3 Turn in the corners, tack all around the edges and then sew with a machine.

4 Fold the napkin into quarters to find the center and sew on a decorative button.

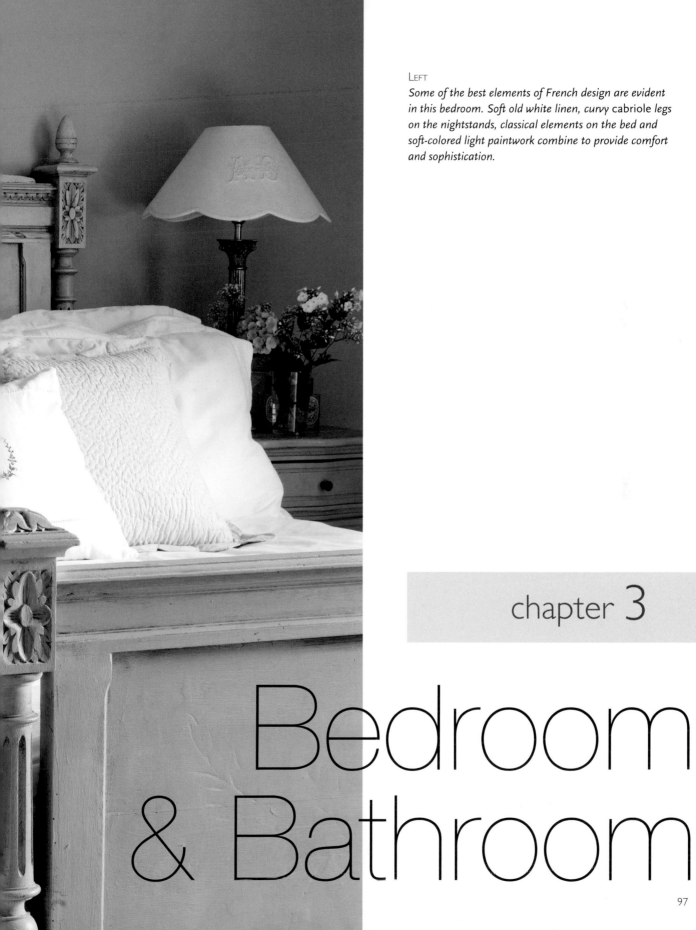

Some of the best elements of French design are evident in this bedroom. Soft old white linen, curvy cabriole legs on the nightstands, classical elements on the bed and soft-colored light paintwork combine to provide comfort and sophistication.

chapter 3

Bedroom
& Bathroom

Château

A bedroom in a beautiful French château conjures up romantic images of a boudoir decorated in soft colors with delicate furniture, swathed in light and flowing fabrics. This is the inspiration of Madame de Pompadour, the powerful mistress of Louis XV, who made her mark on both French culture and interior decorating with her exquisite taste and intellect. She introduced the idea of femininity into design, and in particular the boudoir, creating a room that was more than a bed chamber—it was a private place where a woman could relax. Indeed the word boudoir comes from *bouder*, meaning to sulk— perhaps the word was used as a non-threatening way of getting away from the menfolk.

Rococo Extravagance

The typical rococo bed has a rounded curvy headboard with a central, carved asymmetrical shell-like motif repeated on the center of the sides. The footboard is a smaller copy of the headboard. In high château style the bed would also be painted and gilded to match the paneled walls. Shell white, ivory, dove gray, and sugar almond pinks and blues contrasted with moldings in warm gold. A dressing table that was more like a small bureau with drawers and an opening lid, a small *canapé*, *bergere* chairs and decorative gilded mirrors would often complete the room. This was essentially a very pretty room made grander with flowery toiles and finest silks.

The rococo era came to an end towards the last part of the 18th century and in its place came a return of a more minimal and architectural look. This period has given us the distinctive and still popular sleigh, or boat-shape, bed. Like so much French design its creation was influenced by a woman. The wife of a rich and influential banker commissioned Louis Berthault to design her house, which he did with Greco-Roman friezes and wall panels, marble floors, and mahogany furniture. The boat-shaped bed he designed for her was made of solid mahogany. It had straight sides and scroll top, decorated with sculpted bronze swans and gilt-bronze mounts. Over this a circular

LEFT
This side table epitomizes French style—it is simple and practical but has graceful, delicate, and discrete lines.

coronet was suspended from the ceiling and hung with creamy white fabric that had been decorated with stars along the leading edge. Napoleon's bed in the Château de Malmaison in Paris was more like a daybed with firm tubular bolsters either end and an upturned "V" shape of white striped fabric draped over the bed's sides. If rococo was feminine, this design style was definitely masculine.

What we see nowadays is an amalgamation of the rococo and later neo-classical designs—charming, painted carved beds with coronet drapes, and painted sleigh beds with attractive fabrics. To go with this, keep curtains simple. Use vintage, or modern, linens, or even silks, with a bold decorative braid along the leading edge.

Country

Although the bedroom in the *manoir* is more restrained and less grand than the one found in the château, it is still very appealing and has been much copied all over the world. Beds, both reproduction and vintage, are available in many styles. Carved, rococo bedheads decorated with small flowers or a simple curlicue, painted and distressed in soft colors, look charming. The *Directoire* typically has a triangular shape with a raised urn in the center, although others combine straight and curved lines. Some curved and upholstered bedheads have wooden carved molding, like *bergere* chairs. If you want something unusual,

consider using a piece of paneling from an *armoire* as a bedhead, or use one of the many coronets on the market, either one that has a straightforward band of metal or a more elaborate flowery version.

ORIGINAL BEDLINEN

The art of bed making in France is, like many other things, subtly different from other parts of Europe. Duvets are unpopular, and the French like to use a *traversin*—a long bolster pillow that runs the width of the bed against the bedhead in front of which will be square pillows, either all in

This original bed is from the Directoire period at the end of the 18th century when design was becoming more architectural and classical. It has been upholstered in natural linen studded around the edges. On the bed is a lovely old tasseled pillow with appliquéd pieces of embroidered linen and ticking. The room's furniture has been painted in olive green and various whites, then waxed to give a patina of age. The beams have been painted in white to tone with the very soft pink plaster, so as not to interrupt the classical lines of the bed and the lamp base.

white or in different but toning colors. The French tend to sleep between two sheets with a blanket and third sheet over the top, with a quilt for warmth. Nightstands or bedside tables do not have to match. The tables, or *chevets*, may be of a similar design but one will often be large with a marble top, the other plain and small.

Curtains are kept light and unstructured. As shutters are used throughout France on the outside of the house, there is little need for heavy fabric. A simple, floppy heading, or small, ungathered heading, on linen curtains looks very natural and pretty.

Provençal

LEFT
Several elements of a typical Provençal bedroom are displayed here—the floor is tiled, there is an old and distressed wooden rush-seated bench for two, and on the lovely four poster, wrought-iron bed lies an appliquéd and quilted bedcover.

RIGHT
Light voile curtains protect the room from the heat and glare of the sun.

The Provençal bedroom is a light and airy affair. A wrought-iron four poster bed, hung with translucent fabric that has been loosely tied at the top, is a main feature. It stands on a stone or tiled floor. Light, summery fabrics at shuttered windows keep out winter drafts and turn the simplest country design into a sophisticated look.

THE TRADITIONAL *BOUTIS*

A traditional bedroom in Provence, perhaps on the coast around Marseilles, would have a snowy white *boutis*, or thin quilt, on the bed in pride of place. This scalloped-edged quilt, decorated with all sorts of intricate raised patterns from stripes to trailing leaves, pineapples, and flowers, is the lighter summer cover for the bed and would have been made by the women in the family. Traditional sewing methods, sometimes called Marseilles or Marcella embroidery, are still practiced and it is possible to learn how to make these beautiful quilts. Nowadays, all sorts of *boutis* are available in every colour and pattern. Traditionally used fabrics, called *indienne*, came from India and China, via Marseilles, and are now what many people identify with Provence. They have small flowery or paisley patterns in off-beat colors, such as combinations of yellow ochers, tomato red, and bottle green. Use a *boutis* with several pillows to match for the bed and chairs, and reflect these colors in the bathroom.

The popularity of wrought ironwork in Provence is probably a result of the region's proximity to Spain, where craftsmanship with metal reached a pinnacle. Bedsteads are often painted in sandy grays and soft gray greens, and a painted metalwork chandelier or lantern is also part of the Provençal look. Search for them in flea markets, along with fold-away single beds, cots, and daybeds as well as marble-topped tables that can be used in the bathroom

White is the obvious choice for Provence, enhanced by the colors of the area. Paint walls in fresh pale olive greens and woodwork in lavender blues, and match these with white-painted furniture and fabrics. For a tropical Cote d'Azur style, choose a brighter colored *boutis* for the bedroom.

ALTERNATIVE LOOK

A more rustic image of Provence was immortalized by Van Gogh in his painting of his bedroom in Arles. The floor is wood and the single bed is chunky and wooden. A row of hooks is fixed low down on the wall for hanging clothes and the room is furnished with plain rush-seated chairs. There are no curtains at the window, just shutters to keep out the strong sun. The walls are a soft pale blue. Use lavender everywhere, of course, in the bedroom and bathroom, for its relaxing properties.

Parisian

The drama of *haute couture* and the fashion world is never far away from interior design in Paris. Jeanne Lanvin, one of the most influential fashion designers in the 1920s, even developed an interior design section to her business in her later years. At the Musée des Arts Décoratifs in Paris, some rooms from her apartment have been reproduced to show her innovative and bold style.

RADICAL BATHROOMS

Jeanne Lanvin's bathroom and bedroom are inspirational for their radical, chic, and fashion-led approach. The bathroom is a supreme example of art deco, with white walls, black metalwork, and black, white, and beige marble set in triangular shapes. The bath itself is oval and made from marble.

Lanvin's bedroom is lined in vivid blue silk, the color found in Italian Renaissance paintings, and embroidered with white daisies, roses, and palms in honor of her daughter Marguerite.

Be inspired by these bold statements and make your Parisian bedroom and bathroom extravagant, drawing on ideas, materials, and colors from the France's rich decorating past. For instance, there are now wonderful cheeky new French designers who have brought *toile de Jouy* up to date with zebras and highwaymen, teddy bears and the Eiffel tower. Line the walls of your bedroom with fabric, have a four-poster bed with fabric hangings, and include chandeliers and large, gilded, ornate mirrors.

RIGHT

This antithesis of a modern, fully fitted bathroom has the feel of a room that just happens to have a bath in it. The mood is set by the blue glass chandelier, which immediately draws our attention, and enhanced by an eclectic array of French objects, including the marble-topped chiffonier, the statue, and the neo-classical urn positioned over the far mirror.

LEFT

The slightly saucy 1920s poster advertising a seaside resort in the north of France, when coupled with the old French glass lampshade, the painting and the little cabinets, gives this bathroom a Parisian look and nostalgic appeal.

curtain pole

Curtain poles are often integral to the look of a room, especially a bedroom, and should not be neglected. Here a beautiful wooden pole has been painted to display ornate, French, 19th-century, brass, acanthus-leaf design curtain rings. The painting technique described can be used on any small wooden item where a dragged or stringed effect is wanted.

YOU WILL NEED
Curtain pole
250 ml mid-tone paint
Brushes
100 ml neutral tone paint
250 ml clear wax
Cloth

1 Paint a wooden curtain pole in a mid-tone color, such as Château Grey.

2 Next, brush on a layer of thinned-down paint in a soft neutral putty color, such as Country Grey.

3 While still damp, carefully wipe off the second layer with a damp cloth so the paint is gently streaked. When dry, apply two layers of wax. Polish the pole on the second day to ensure the rings run smoothly.

vintage linen curtains

YOU WILL NEED
Old embroidered sheets
Scissors
Needle and cotton
Sewing machine
Pins
Strip of thicker fabric
(optional)
Curtain heading

If you have a suitably sized window, beautiful old French linen sheets can make unusual curtains. The linen should allow for the window drop plus at least 6 in. (15 cm) for the heading. Old sheets are often a warm, creamy white and can sometimes be found with delicately embroidered monograms. Finding an identical pair will be difficult, so you may have to compromise with two that are similar. The curtains can hang from either a big, floppy, untailored heading or a stiffer, ruffle.

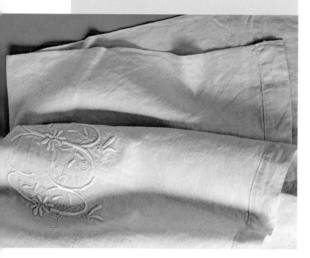

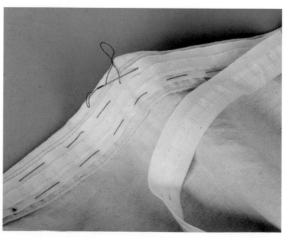

2 To give strength and weight to the top of the curtain, cut a 3 in. (7.5 cm) strip of fabric from the bottom of the sheet, hem it and sew it on to the top of the sheet. You will then have to re-hem the bottom. Alternatively, use a separate piece of suitable cotton fabric.

1 On a vintage sheet, the monogram usually lies at the foot of the bed, in the center, so that it can be read as you look at the bed. To turn the sheet into a curtain with the monogram at the top, fold the monogrammed end over so there is a large overhang.

3 Pin, tack, and sew a heading for a gathered curtain along the top of the sheet.

Alternative uses:
The voile used to make these curtains is a mix of linen and cotton—a translucent fabric that also has texture and a good weight. Instead of sewing the heading tape to the top of the curtain, position it about 4 in. (10 cm) down, so that the ruffle extends over the curtain rings.

4 Pull up the gathers of the curtain until the fabric is the right width and spaced as you want it. Tie the heading threads. Pull the fabric out a little in the center, where the embroidery falls, so that the detail can be clearly seen.

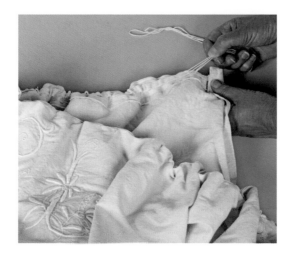

a country *armoire*

This typical Louis XI style *armoire* has a removable *chapeau* and base, and the door is made without hinges—two pins in the top and base fit into corresponding holes. When I found it in a flea market, it had been partly repainted and in the door was a mirror that had been added at a later date. Removing the mirror revealed dark creamy paintwork, which inspired the color scheme for its renovation—a pale brown putty color with white for the raised moldings. Patination was added with dark and clear waxes.

YOU WILL NEED

Country Grey Chalk Paint

Old White Chalk Paint

Paint brushes

Artist's brush (small)

Clear wax

Very fine sandpaper

Dark wax

Lint-free cloth

LEFT & RIGHT
Transforming a run-down old armoire into a useful wardrobe is very satisfying, and this one makes a delightful addition to a country-style bedroom. The old hooks have been kept and a bar added. Note that it is not essential for armoires to have shelves to be authentic.

a country *armoire*

1 Apply two layers of a soft water based paint so that the original paint is completely covered. Move the brush in different directions as you paint, rather than just up and down, to create a little texture. This is so that, when you apply the darker wax in step 5, the texture will show and help to give the surface a patina.

2 Allow to dry then, using an artist's brush, paint a not-too-bright white over the moldings. This does not have to be done very carefully. It is best to lay the brush on its side, applying the paint in a wiping action, rather than trying to delineate and cover the whole molding.

3 Dip the brush into the clear wax so that it is well covered—this is helpful for reaching into all the nooks and crannies of the raised moldings. The aim is for the wax to soak into the paint, not to create a layer of thick wax.

4   Use a piece of very fine sandpaper to rub gently over the surface, particularly over the edges and moldings. Remove the paint entirely to reveal the wood in some places and, in others, just rub off the white to reveal the brown gray underneath.

5   Apply the dark wax, concentrating on the edges and moldings. Use a scrubbing motion so that the wax sinks into all the brush lines and into any indentations in the wood. Spread the wax thinly and avoid creating any areas of thick wax.

6   Using a soft cotton cloth, such as on old sheet, well dipped into clear wax, wipe over the surface of the *armoire*. Keep a clean cloth ready to wipe off the excess.

alternative uses

The same technique can be used on all sorts of furniture with more layers and many different colors. Chalk paint absorbs wax easily so the final result can be buffed to create a soft shine.

country washed wood

On the cool, tiled floor of a country bedroom, the warmth of wood can add the perfect finishing touch. Here the washed wood of the chair and mirror contrast also with the chunky painted table and the natural wood of the birdcage. Using this technique allows the grain of the wood to show through and the effect is faded and very soft.

1 Find furniture made from porous wood that has not been varnished. Dip a sponge dampened with water into slightly diluted water based paint and wipe it over the wood. Take care in the corners that you don't get a build up of paint. You might need another sponge to smooth these areas away.

YOU WILL NEED
2 sponges
100 ml water based paint
Cloth

2 Depending on how much wood you want to show through, wipe off the excess paint with a cloth. The wood grain is quite well defined on this chair and the white paint helps to bring it out. The mirror in the background has less paint taken off as the wood has few markings on it.

provençal coronet bedhead

YOU WILL NEED

Coronet

100 ml Old White Chalk Paint

Paintbrush

Fabric for hangings

Needle and cotton

Pins

The fabric used here is of a cotton linen mix, decorated with cicadas, the motif of the South of France. It is loosely tied to the decorative semi-circular coronet with tapes, in typical Provençal style.

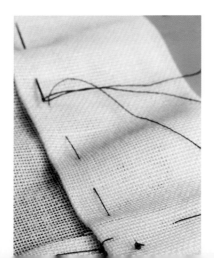

1 First, paint the metal coronet in Old White. The idea is to avoid working paint into the recesses, so being careful not to overload the brush, use its edges, rather than just the tip, to cover just the raised areas of the flowers and leaves.

2 Measure the fabric for the hangings, allowing double the width of the coronet plus the drop to the floor. Include extra for hems top and bottom. Fold, iron, pin, and tack the edges of the fabric.

3 Neatly hem top and bottom. Make sure the hems are not too large, especially if the foldovers are obvious. Here the hem is about 2 in. (5 cm) deep.

4 For the tapes, cut lengths of the same fabric at least 24 in. (60 cm) long and 2 in. (5 cm) wide. Fold them in half, right sides facing, sew along the length and turn inside out. Tack the center of each tape to the hanging, evenly spaced.

117

provençal
lavender heart

Toile de Jouy and a striped fabric combine well in this sweet lavender-filled heart. Use tracing paper to isolate the scene you want to emphasize on the front of the heart and take care to include a loop of ribbon to use as a hanger.

You will need
Tracing paper and pencil
Scissors
Toile de Jouy and a matching fabric
Needle and cotton
Pins
Ribbon
Batting to fill
Lavender

1 Draw and cut out the shape of a heart on tracing paper. Then make a second template for the part of the heart in striped fabric, adding 1 in. (2.5 cm) along the straight edge. Pin the templates to the fabric and cut out both shapes.

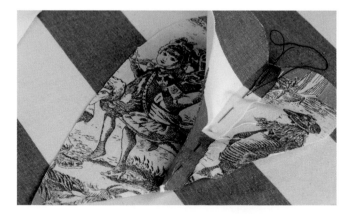

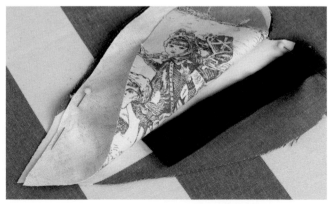

2 Pin the striped fabric onto on heart shape, right sides facing, so that it is in the correct position when folded out. Pin, tack, and sew the seam, making certain you have a neat straight line.

3 With the stripy second half folded out, place the two heart shapes right sides facing. Cut a piece of ribbon, fold it in half then place it inside the heart, tacking in place as shown.

4   To make sure the heart doesn't pucker when you turn it right side out, snip the fabric around the top arcs. Sew the two heart shapes together, leaving a gap along one side of about 2 in. (5 cm).

5   Turn the heart right side out and stuff it with some batting or cotton wool and some fresh lavender heads either from the yard or from a store.

alternative uses

Enlarge the heart to use as a small pillow, capitalizing on the relaxing properties of lavender. To give a more rustic feel, replace the batting with wheat and use a plain linen decorated with little buttons or braid.

gathered skirt lampshade

YOU WILL NEED
Lampshade frame
Double-sided tape
Scissors
Cream cotton lining fabric
Fabric adhesive
Cotton bias binding
Pins
Sewing machine
15 1/2 in. (40 cm) of main fabric
Cotton thread
1 yd. (1 m) elastic thread
Large sewing needle
1 yd. (1 m) ribbon

This lampshade was inspired by urban fashion of the 1950s—gathered skirts that were often tied with a ribbon at the top. Choose a soft, light fabric that hangs well, such as the linen and cotton mix used here. A vintage fabric that has lost all its stiffening would also work. well, and give a different look. The collared lampshade—which is available from specialist makers—needs to be covered with a plain backing fabric so that the light is not too bright or harsh. The amount of fabric you need will probably be more than you initially think. Instructions are for a 8½ in. (22 cm) high lampshade. The diameter is 5⅔ in. (15 cm) at the top, increasing to 11 in. (28 cm) at the bottom.

1 Cover the top and bottom circles of the frame with some strong double-sided tape. Remove the backing from the tape when you are ready to begin covering the lampshade.

ABOVE & LEFT
The soft linen check fabric and burgundy velvet ribbon give the shade a demure look. By using outrageous and vintage retro fabrics, you could make it look more boho chic or jazzy. Spotted, striped or vintage braid or ribbon could be used with a plain fabric. This velvet ribbon is wide enough to cover the knot when tied around the shade.

gathered skirt lampshade

2 Cut approximately 12 in. (30 cm) of the cream cotton lining material and, leaving the first ³/8 in. (1 cm) free, start sticking the fabric around the bottom ring. Also leave about 1 in. (2.5 cm) at the end to act as a positioning guide. This is later trimmed off. Tuck in the end of your fabric underneath the flap left at the beginning. Stretch the fabric to the top of the frame and stick in place, pleating as you go to take account of the smaller circle. When you have finished, apply a small dab of strong clear fabric adhesive under each pleat then trim off the excess fabric, top and bottom.

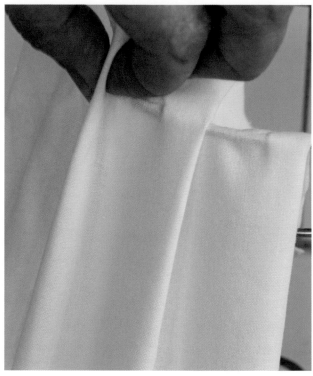

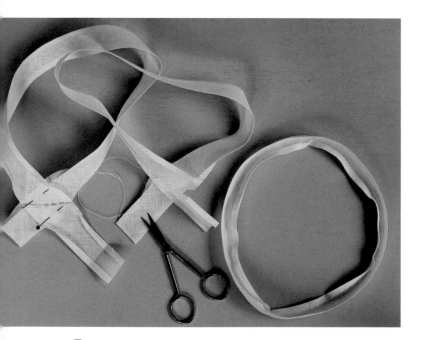

3 To cover and neaten the two top rings and the bottom of the frame, wind cotton bias binding around the circumference of one of the top rings. Allowing about 2 in. (5 cm) excess, secure with a pin, then machine sew straight across the crossover (shown in the red line above). Make a second ring for the collared area. Repeat a third time, making a larger ring for the bottom of the frame. Secure the bias binding rings in place with strong fabric adhesive.

4 Join the seam of the main fabric, making a circle and overlapping to neaten the edge.

5   Turn over ³/₄ in. (2 cm) for the top edge and press, then turn again allowing a 2 in. (5 cm) hem, pin, and press. Stitch along the bottom edge of the hem, reverse stitching to secure the end of the stitching line. To make a channel for the elasticated thread, stitch a second row about ¹/₂ in. (1 cm) up from the first, reverse stitching again at the end.

6   Make a deeper bottom hem for the skirt, allowing an extra 1 ³/₄ in. (4 cm) in length so that it hangs over the edge of the metal lampshade. Press the skirt well.

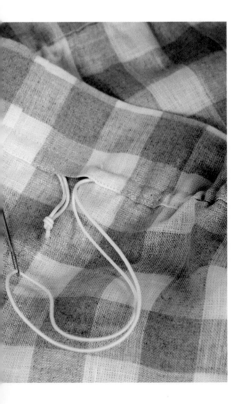

7   Thread a large needle with the elasticated thread and push it through the channel, then draw up the gathers as tightly as possible to fit around the smaller ring. Knot the ends securely and cut off the excess elastic. Push the knot into the channel opening.

8   Tie a length of ribbon of your choice around the lampshade and knot in place.

 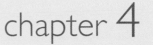
Garden
Room

A beautiful, old, and very large marble fire surround found in an architectural reclamation yard has been put to ingenious use as a garden console table. Even a partly broken fireplace can be placed along a garden wall like this, because any flaws can easily be disguised with judicious planting.

Château

The garden of the French château is particularly formal. It is geometric and symmetrical and, to appreciate the shapes, it is best seen from a high window. The style is derived from medieval knot gardens, where flowers were contained in shapely borders edged with rows of hedging. The French developed a more architectural form of the knot garden, called the *parterre*, by creating interlocking shapes using only green box plants. Simple rectangles and maze-like plantings evolved into arabesques and rococo curlicue designs. Plants with different colored leaves were used to enhance the pattern, giving an effect from above of raised green embroidery. From the ground shapely topiary hedges were visible in the form of cones, pyramids, and spheres. There were very few flowers; instead, geometrically shaped lakes and fountains along with tall classical statuary gave grandeur. This was the taming of the countryside, in spite of the French love of nostalgic pastoral scenes on their fabrics.

FORMAL SPLENDOR

This neo-classical architectural style is the form of gardening that has triumphed in France and the formality was echoed in the garden room. The greatest example of combining garden and room is to be seen at Versailles. Claude Mollet developed the formal *parterre* in the 18th century and it was used at Versailles under the guidance of André Le Nôtre, who designed and laid out the gardens. His designs included an orangery, a building somewhere between a garden room and a sunroom, where exotic warmth-loving fruit, such as, oranges were grown.

LEFT
Handfuls of hazelnuts are thrown among neo-classical raised stars, which were used for furniture decoration. It is traditional to gather the fruit and nuts that grow wild in the château gardens.

*In a garden room, an intriguing collection
of neo-classical architectural pieces sits on
an old French metal-framed table. The
various objects are laid out symmetrically,
in keeping with the formal parterres of
the château, but there is a touch of
whimsy here with the old garden hats, the
hazelnuts, and the wire basket of shells.*

Country

The *manoir* garden is as like the garden of Versailles as the owner could make it—formal and symmetrical, filled with greenery and possibly a few architectural features. Often this would simply be a tall front wall with an imposing main gate opening on to a central, straight path or driveway leading to the front of an equally symmetrical house.

There may be rows of trees and gravel pathways but never more than a few flowers. While low boxwood hedges might develop into *parterres,* any trees would be vigorously pruned so that they can be kept in the right architectural form. Yews, box trees, hornbeams, and cypress trees were popular species because they could be easily pruned and shaped.

The Kitchen Garden
Behind the house would be the most important area—the kitchen garden, where all the vegetables and fruit for the house would be grown. This would be kept in the same symmetrical and well-ordered manner as the rest of the garden.

The more rustic your own yard, the more suitable it becomes as a kitchen plot. Fruit trees—such as apples, pears, and a variety of plums and greengages, including the French "Reine Claude"—are the trees of the north. Farther south they are replaced by vineyards.

Of course, the French countryman loves flowers too but they will usually be confined to those needing little attention. His heart and mind will be with the plants that can provide good flavors for his table. One of the most robust and popular flowers is the ubiquitous brilliant red or pink geranium, as any journey through France will indicate—they can be seen in window boxes and pots in every village and farmyard. Hydrangeas are probably the second most popular plant. These thrive on the shady side of the house and by water. Lily-of-the-valley is an old favorite and will often be found in French country gardens. It is traditionally handed out at special events, and its sweet perfume makes it very popular for bridal arrangements.

Use ginghams and flowery fabrics, metal tables and chairs with delightful curvy backs and arms. Kitchen enamelware is simply brought out into the garden when eating outdoors.

Provençal

The difference in climate between the north and the south of France is quite significant. A Provençal garden revolves around lavender, herbs, and sunflowers, olive trees and grapevines. In more northerly climates, an indoor garden room with under-floor heating ensures that at least some of these plants can be accommodated even in the coldest temperatures.

Use gravel in the garden with big terra cotta pots, painted chairs and tables, and soft fabrics. Have big shutters on the outside of the house and paint them the beautiful fresh blue or green you find in the Mediterranean, perhaps against an ocher-colored wall. The kitchen garden remains important, with basil and rosemary to go with tomatoes, peppers, and all the other Mediterranean vegetables.

PROVENÇAL INSPIRATION

For inspiration, discover the garden of olive trees and orange groves at the artist Renoir's home in the South of France. Another impressionist, Claude Monet, had a famous house and garden in Giverny, near Paris. Despite being in the north, both the house and garden were inspired by Provence. To bring out the shades of the garden and to make it appear bright and colorful, Monet used combinations of complementary colors, so wherever there is an orange there is also a blue, and purple lavender or iris is matched with nearby yellow or orange companion plants. The house is painted pink with green shutters and woodwork, just as if it was in Provence.

The nearer the Cote d'Azur the more exotic the planting can be. Oranges and lemons, figs, avocado, bananas, and palm trees grow alongside bright colored flowers, including purple bougainvillea and pink weigela. Many shrubs and trees have gray green leaves, indicating the lack of rain in the area. In your Provençal garden room, reflect these Mediterranean color in napkins and tablecloths, and in the color you paint your furniture.

ABOVE
This old oak table has been out in the garden for years, and is alternately soaked with rain and dried out in the sun. Now bleached gray, the wood's beautiful patina suits the dry, smoky colors of lavender, rosemary, and sage.

,BELOW & LEFT
Create the Riviera look with bright striped pillows and palm fronds. Vibrant purples and pinks are the colors of creeping bougainvillea. Combined with the azure blue of the sea these are great colors for napkins. Spots and stripes conjure up the carefree outdoor life of the south of France.

Parisian

In Paris, greenery and flowers nestle in quite unexpected places. Trees poke out over rooftops, large window boxes overflow with greenery, and glass-covered balconies are filled with tropical abundance. Peek through elegant open doors while wandering the streets of Paris to catch a glimpse of perfect little courtyard gardens with formal planting in stone pots. Bay trees cut in the shape of cones or balls are a wonderful way of embellishing a small courtyard garden. A stone bench, statue or small fountain inset into the wall are not unusual. These formal areas take inspiration from the city's historic gardens, such as the Jardin des Tuileries, first laid out with elegant and symmetrical *parterres* by the same gardener who designed Versailles. Dine outside in the evenings with candelabra on a white tablecloth.

COUNTRY IN THE CITY

A Parisian garden contains a little of every French style. The countryside is brought into the city with shapely wooden benches and simple pillows. Find pots and tubs for herbs and climbing vegetables, such as French beans. Paint odd containers, such as old tins and watering cans, then fill them with red geraniums and hydrangeas. Fill wall-mounted wire planters with pots and search flea markets for reproductions of the traditional freestanding wrought-iron planters. Bohemian chic is never far away in Paris. Paint a cupboard for your garden tools and mix French country style with urns and mirrors for an *haute couture* look.

Bring the aroma of Provence into your garden with big pots of lavender and lemon verbena. Grow Provençal culinary plants such as tarragon, basil, and rosemary. Put gravel down to give the feeling and sound of the Luberon. An olive tree, if sheltered and in a sunny position, will thrive and provide the appropriate shade of gray green. A grapevine, given enough sun and a big enough pot, will grow brilliantly and may even bear fruit. With candles in lanterns at night you will be transported to Provence.

rattan furniture painting

In France, rattan and bamboo furniture would have been painted white or in pale summery colors and set out in a garden room or orangery. Due to its rough surface, it is not quick to paint so, before you start, decide if you are going to cover the piece or just skate over the surface—here you can still see bamboo peeping through. A favorite method of the 18th century was painting seats in a checkered pattern. I have used three colors—a duck-egg blue base, a blue green, and finally white. This sort of chair looks quite at home in a smart garden room.

YOU WILL NEED
Wood adhesive
100 ml two colored
Chalk Paints
Large paintbrush
100 ml Old White
Chalk Paint

1 First mend any of the fine rattan strands that are broken by gluing them in place. Paint the chair in Duck Egg Blue with the tip of the brush, working over the same area several times. Each time you recharge your brush, put the first dollop of paint on an area bound with rattan as this will take more paint and help to create even coverage.

2 Paint the seat base in alternate stripes of Duck Egg Blue and Château Grey, allowing each to dry thoroughly before proceeding with the next color.

3 Finish with a stripe of white painted in the opposite direction, leaving gaps of equal width between each stripe to allow the crossing stripes to show through.

country-style pillows

YOU WILL NEED

Selection of fabric remnants

Scissors

Pins

Needle and cotton

Zipper

Pillow forms

It is the odd symmetry of the *toile de Jouy* fabrics that makes these pillows so charming. Collect left-over pieces of fabric or find remnants and base the color of your pillow on the central design—the pastoral scenes of *toile de Jouy* give an excellent focus. There are two pillow designs here—one with five panels using four fabrics, the other with nine panels and five fabrics. Surrounding the patterned fabrics are at least two that are plain or have a simple stripe or check, while an outer strip adds a contrasting pattern.

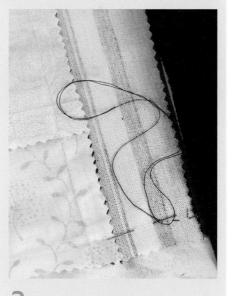

1 Find a collection of fabric pieces that work together in color and design. These pillows use a *toile de Jouy* fabric in the center, with stripes, although plain or abstract patterns could equally well have been used.

2 Cut out the pieces of fabric in either square or rectangular shapes, just as you wish, with an overlap of about 2 in. (2.5 cm), and then pin them together.

3 Fold over the edges and, working from the back, tack then sew the pieces of fabric together. Join the patchwork to a plain piece of fabric for the reverse of the pillow, fixing a zipper down one edge.

pigment painted chair

YOU WILL NEED

2 tsp pigment

Spoon and bowl

250 ml thick natural yogurt

Medium paintbrush

Making paint using yogurt or curdled milk as a binding agent for pigment is an old, rural technique for putting a glut of milk to good use. The first thought is that it will smell, go moldy or come off on your clothes but, in fact, none of these things occur and, in the right mixture, the paint is completely stable. This chair was painted with a deep green pigment some years ago and has aged and distressed in an extremely lovely way without being varnished or waxed.

2   Add the yogurt to the pigment and stir around with the spoon until the mixture has a smooth consistency and can be applied with a brush. The yogurt is the adhesive that binds the paint together, making it stick to the furniture.

1   Put the pigment in a bowl and break it down into a fine powder with a spoon. The exact quantities of both pigment and yoghurt are difficult to give as each pigment is of a different strength.

3   Test the mixture on a small hidden area of the chair to see how stable it is when it dries—since the paint is so basic, it will take a very short time to dry. If that works, then paint the rest of the chair. Not using primer will result in the wood looking distressed and worn almost immediately.